Praise for

"*The Dog and the Dentist Chair* is filled with
beautiful stories of hope, love and compassion
to support the powerful bond between children
and animals. This book is paw-tastic!"

—ROBIN GANZERT,
President and Chief Executive Officer of American Humane

"Peggy Frezon loves animals. More than that,
she also understands children.
While *The Dog and the Dentist Chair* is full of touching
true stories of animals and kids together,
it's Peggy's heartfelt empathy and friendly voice
that makes them shine."

—ALINE ALEXANDER NEWMAN,
National Geographic author of *How to Speak Dog* and
How to Speak Cat

"With great warmth Peggy Frezon shows young people that companion animals can be more than companions. They can also be our guides, bringing us to greater kindness, courage, and well being."

—GAYLE BOSS,
Author of *All Creation Waits*

"*The Dog in the Dentist Chair* is also valuable for an adult reader. It's an inspiring resource for parents, teachers, and caregivers looking for ways to reach and heal the children in their care."

—MELINDA JOHNSON,
Author of *Piggy in Heaven*

"I loved all the marvelous animals Peggy Frezon writes about in this book. Her engaging style is every bit as kid-friendly as the stories she tells. This will make children smile, cuddle up, and be comforted and inspired, even as they learn wonderful things about our animal friends. Highly recommended!"

—M.R. WELLS, coauthor of
Four Paws from Heaven and *The Cat Lover's Devotional*

The Dog
in the
Dentist
Chair

And Other
True Stories
of Animals
Who Help,
Comfort, and
Love Kids

PEGGY FREZON

PARACLETE PRESS
BREWSTER, MASSACHUSETTS

2019 First Printing

The Dog and the Dentist Chair: And Other True Stories of Animals Who Help, Comfort, and Love Kids

Photo credits: Amanda Arnold (Oliver-horse by trailer), Shannon Barry (Spencer and Sheldon), Bunnies in Baskets (Tess), Abby Chesnut (Oliver-rat), Kara Chrisman (Molly and little boy), Keith Comer (Cloud), Lindsay Condefer (Lentil), Jaclyn Egger (JoJo with blonde girl), Steve Frederick (Oliver-horse), Mike Frezon (Bacon Bits, Murfy at airport, Murfy with teen boy, Blue on books), Judy Fridono (Cori), Gentle Carousel (Magic), Green Chimneys (Sage), Dayna Hilton (Molly), Terry Hutchison (Bacon Bits), Barb Kelp (Blue on Legos), Kelli McDonald (Gracie), Deb Moreland (Harley), Katrina Matuszak-Haskell (Murfy), Sarah Morr (Raul), Rob Ochoa (Ricochet), Jamie Richter (Indy), Lynn Ryan (JoJo), Tracey Shearer (Parfait), Candice Shepherd (Monty), Sherri Shultz (Reggie)

Scriptures are taken from The Holy Bible, Easy-to-Read Version, Copyright © 1987, 1999, 2006 Bible League International. All rights reserved.

The Paraclete Press name and logo (dove on cross) are trademarks of Paraclete Press, Inc.

Library of Congress Cataloging-in-Publication Data is available.

10 9 8 7 6 5 4 3 2 1

Published by Paraclete Press
Brewster, Massachusetts
www.paracletepress.com

Printed in the United States of America

To the kids and animals in my life:
Grace and Lily and Ernest and Petey

So God made
every kind of animal.
He made the wild animals, the
tame animals, and all the small
crawling things.
And God saw that
this was good.

—GENESIS 1:25

Contents

The Dog in the Dentist Chair

1
JoJo

JoJo stretches her furry paws atop a long, reclining chair. Above her shines a bright light. In front of her sits a tray with a toothbrush and toothpaste, a little sink and a paper cup.

You probably wouldn't expect to see a dog at the dentist's. But JoJo isn't there to get her teeth cleaned. This dentist office is for kids.

Some boys and girls love visiting the dentist. They know that it keeps their teeth and gums healthy. They even enjoy the minty taste of the toothpaste. Or it may be berry or bubblegum flavored—it's fun when you get a choice. But some other kids get nervous when they go to the dentist. They hold their breath when the dentist asks them to open their mouth. They cover their ears at the whirring sound of the polisher. *What's going to happen next? Is it going to hurt?*

One day, a little girl with a cavity visits the dentist. She feels worried. She doesn't want to have her teeth checked at all. She shakes her head and presses her lips tightly together. "No," she says, trembling. She won't even climb into the dentist chair. She just sniffles and clings to her mom and dad.

"I know who can help," the hygienist says. She leaves the room and returns with a happy golden dog on a leash. The dog actually looks as if she is smiling. Her formal name is JoJo Comfort Dog. She wears a special blue vest so everyone knows that she is a working dog. She also wears a purple collar and a purple bandana. The girl smiles too, because purple is her favorite color. "Do you want JoJo to sit next to you, or in your lap?"

JoJo wags her tail. Her chocolate-brown eyes are bright and friendly. She has a way of making children relax. The girl's hands stop shaking. "In my lap," she answers. The hygienist puts a blue blanket over the dentist chair. The little girl slowly climbs up. Then, just like that, JoJo jumps onto the chair, too.

JoJo settles against the girl's legs. The girl reaches down and pats JoJo's golden fur. She doesn't even realize that the dentist has already begun working on her teeth. Once,

JoJo the comfort
dog

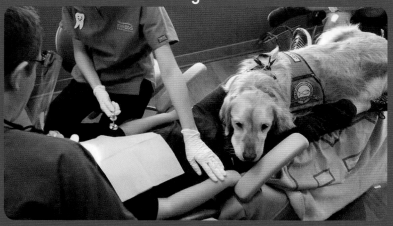

JoJo

BREED: Golden Retriever

AGE: 7 years

COLOR: golden-yellow

WEIGHT: 70 lbs.

FAVORITE FOOD: dog food

FAVORITE TOY: tennis ball

LIVES IN: Illinois

when a tool makes a loud noise, she starts to squirm. JoJo puts her paw on the girl's lap. The weight of the dog's paw helps keep fidgety arms and legs from wiggling. Patting the soft, warm dog helps the girl stay calm. Before she knows it, the appointment is over. It wasn't so bad after all. She climbs out of the chair and hugs JoJo goodbye. "Good job," the dentist says. "JoJo and I will see you again next time."

JoJo works with many children who are afraid of the dentist. When her work is done, she strolls off to the kitchen break room, where she takes a drink from her own bowl of water. The dental hygienists sit down for lunch. JoJo doesn't beg. She likes hugs instead of treats. Good thing there are plenty of hugs to go around.

Soon it is time to go home. Like most dogs, JoJo lives in a house with a family. She runs and plays outside in her yard. She goes on walks. She eats her dog food—no table scraps for JoJo.

Some days JoJo's human mom buckles JoJo into her bright blue vest. The patch on the vest says "Lutheran Church Charities Comfort Dog." This means that JoJo is specially trained to help make people feel better. When she's wearing the vest, she knows she's going to work. But JoJo doesn't only work at the dentist office—she has other jobs, too. She brings comfort to many boys and girls in need. One way is by visiting schoolkids during Backpack Blessings. Students who don't have their own supplies are given a pack full of pencils, markers, and notebooks. JoJo also loves to help kids read. One time she was listening to a group of Spanish-speaking students practice reading in English. One of the boys decided to teach her Spanish. "*Perro* means dog," he said, trilling his *r*'s. JoJo seemed to like hearing the word *dog* in Spanish.

Some days JoJo doesn't work at all. She eats, chases her favorite tennis ball, and naps. Maybe she dreams about all the special friends she's helped. At night she sleeps at the foot of the bed so she can be close to the people she loves.

Don't be afraid, because the
Lord God, my God, is with you.
He will help you until all
the work is finished.
He will not leave you.
—1 CHRONICLES 28:20

2
Gracie

A tiny, brown, speckled kitten once curled up in the corner of a cage at an animal shelter. Someone gave her away. They didn't see her value. But a kind woman named Kelli did. She brought Gracie home to join her family.

Gracie is a beautiful cat with shades of brown, cream, gold, and black. Gracie also has big paws. Most cats have five toes on each foot. Gracie has six toes on each of her front paws. A cat with extra toes is called *polydactyl*.

Each and every day, Gracie the cat shows how happy she is that she was rescued. She pays it forward with love and affection. She especially cares for all children—active kids, shy kids, noisy kids, silly kids. Each and every one. Gracie loves them all.

One day Kelli noticed her local library's program called Ruff Readers. The program helps elementary schoolers who are having trouble reading or are shy about sounding out words. They can read stories to dogs. Dogs don't judge. Dogs don't care if you can't read well yet. *Gracie would love to be a Ruff Reader*, Kelli thought, *but Gracie can't ruff!* "Why don't you have a program for cats?" she asked.

So, the library added a new program. Ruff Readers *and* Cat Chats. Now Gracie goes to the library to help children read. Children who are afraid of big dogs aren't afraid of a cat. Gracie happily joins them in a monster-sized, red bean-bag chair. Sometimes she looks along at early reader books such as *Fat Cat*, or *Pete the Cat*. Other times she listens to a child's favorite story, such as *Pokemon*. Gracie doesn't mind if the young readers can't pronounce something, or stumble over words. Kids who didn't like to read before are excited to read to Gracie. When they are done, Gracie gives each child a high-five. Well, actually a high-six, because of her extra toes.

When she's not working, she naps on top of her cat tree. When she wants to have fun, she taps Kelli's leg. *Tap tap tap. Play with me.* Her favorite game is fetching toys. Soon it's time to go outside. Gracie wears a harness and a leash,

Gracie the book buddy cat

Gracie

BREED: domestic shorthaired/ tortoiseshell cat

AGE: 2 years

COLOR: brown and black with gold flecks

WEIGHT: 10 lbs.

FAVORITE FOOD: potato chips

FAVORITE TOY: stick with a string and a sparkly toy ball on the end

LIVES IN: Wisconsin

and she and Kelli take long walks together. Sometimes they go for more than a mile. That's a lot of walking, even with extra toes.

Sometimes, instead of walking, Gracie rides in a special stroller made just for cats or small dogs. Once, Kelli was pushing Gracie in her stroller at a farmer's market. They passed rows of fruits, vegetables, and flowers. A family hurried by with three young children. They were trying to rush out, because the youngest one was crying and cranky. *I bet we could cheer him up*, Kelli thought. She unzipped the screen covering the stroller and walked over to the family. "Would you like to meet my cat?"

The mom glanced at the crying boy. "I don't know. . . ."

But the older kids rushed right over and started hugging and patting Gracie. Well, that was just fine with Gracie. She doesn't mind being handled all over. She purred and flicked the tip of her tail. "She's so silky," they said. Gracie has extra-soft fur that feels nice to touch. The littlest boy watched, but he was still sobbing. Finally he went over and ran his hand slowly across Gracie's back.

Gracie didn't get upset by his loud cries. She tilted her head and looked at him as if to say, *What's wrong? Why are you crying?* He looked back at her. Slowly the tears stopped. He wiped his eyes and smiled.

"That's amazing," the mom said. "Thank you, Gracie."

Gracie truly loves all children, but there is one extra-special child in her life. A foster child has come to live with them. Kelli cares for the boy, who has extra needs. Sometimes he makes loud, unfamiliar noises. Whenever he cries out, Gracie comes running. She purrs and cuddles with him until he feels better. They even have a special toy they play with together. It is a stick with a string and a sparkly ball at the end. One night Kelli was rocking the boy and reading him a bedtime story. Gracie jumped right up in their laps. Time for her very own Cat Chat. But the child was tired and crying. Gracie kissed him. He kept crying. So Gracie scampered down the stairs. She returned with something special—the stick toy that they loved to play with. She'd dragged it all the way up the stairs and into his room. *Look, our favorite toy. This will make you feel better.* And it did.

Best friends are always there for you. And Gracie is always ready and waiting to give another child love and her very own, one of a kind, high-six.

Fill us with your love every
morning. Let us be happy and
enjoy our lives.

—Psalm 90:14

3
Reggie

A group of boys and girls sits around a table. A woman stands in front of them, calling out letters. "B-A-L-L." Are the kids having a spelling lesson?

No. The kids are relaxing in a living room, not a classroom. And the woman named Sherri is spelling out a word . . . for a dog. A little white and brown dog tilts his head, listening. He jumps up from his pillow and zips over to a box of toys. He pushes the toys around with his nose until he finds a bright orange ball. "That's it!" says Sherri. "Bring it here."

"He knows how to spell the word *ball*," the kids say. "Good dog, Reggie."

The kids live in a group home. They are not brothers and sisters. But they have one thing in common—they need to live apart from their home and family for a while. Some got into trouble. Some ran away. Some of their parents were not able to take good care of them. Sherri and other adults give them care and support. And Reggie is there to help too.

Reggie roams about the big house, up and down the stairs. He finds some boys sprawled on the sofa, watching television. He squeezes in and finds a good spot. He loves to play hard, but he's also happy to be a couch potato. The kids snuggle up with Reggie. No matter what problems they are going through, Reggie doesn't judge. He always accepts them.

After a while, Reggie goes looking for someone else who needs him. He climbs up the stairs and someone gives him a treat. *Thank you!*

He walks down the hall and gets another treat. *Thank you! Hey, this is pretty good!*

In one of the rooms, Reggie finds a girl sitting on her bed. She is upset and crying. Reggie can't talk to her about her problems. But he can still help. He jumps up and climbs right into her lap. The girl's hands cover her face. Reggie

Reggie the group home dog

Reggie

BREED: Jack Russell Terrier

AGE: 8 years

COLOR: white with a black spot on his side

WEIGHT: 20 lbs.

FAVORITE FOOD: dog biscuits

FAVORITE TOY: orange ball

LIVES IN: New York

nuzzles under her hands. He wiggles close and kisses her. She stops crying and hugs him tight. It's hard to be upset when Reggie kisses you.

Soon, Reggie wanders back down the stairs. How does he know where to go? He just finds whoever needs him. If there's a lap, he sits on it. If there's a game to play, he joins in. He loves to make kids laugh. Once, he met a boy in a wheelchair. The boy couldn't see or hear or walk. He could only move his left arm. Of course, Reggie didn't know that. He just knew that he wanted to play ball. So he trotted up and dropped his sloppy tennis ball into the boy's left hand. Reggie nudged the boy's arm and barked. "Hi, Reggie," the boy said, laughing. He threw the ball. Reggie raced after it, caught it, and put it right back in the boy's left hand. They played together time after time. Maybe the boy thought that there wasn't a lot he could do. But he could throw a ball for Reggie. That made them both happy.

Sometimes Sherri dresses Reggie up in costumes or colorful bandanas. He wears a pumpkin outfit for Halloween and a Santa Claus suit for Christmas. Reggie shows off his new look and makes everyone happy. Even kids who are afraid of most dogs aren't afraid of Reggie when he's dressed in one of his cute costumes.

A group of kids goes outside to play and Reggie runs after them. *Will you throw a ball for me?* he seems to ask. One boy keeps the ball for himself. Reggie barks and runs in a little circle. "Why is he doing that?" the boy asks.

"Because he is frustrated," Sherri says.

"I didn't know dogs get frustrated."

"Yes they do. Just like boys, sometimes."

He nods. "I've got you, Reggie." He throws the ball and Reggie zooms after it, tail flying.

After a lively game of fetch, Reggie has one more friend to visit. He makes his way inside and finds Yoda, an old tiger cat, snoozing in a patch of sunlight. Yoda is one of his very best pals. Reggie eases himself down and rests his chin on Yoda's back. Reggie loves everybody.

Whoever accepts a little child
like this in my name
is accepting me.

—MATTHEW 18:5

4
Magic

Sometimes it's best to slip into a room quietly. But Magic the miniature horse likes to make a big entrance. First, she always has music playing. She even has her own special theme song—"Do You Believe in Magic?". Then, while the children are enjoying the lively beat, she trots in—sideways. Have you ever seen a horse walk sideways? Magic tosses her pretty black mane, and clip clops in with her fancy steps. This gets everyone excited and laughing.

But Magic doesn't entertain at a horse show or an amusement park. She is a therapy horse, and she belongs to an organization called Gentle Carousel Miniature Therapy Horses. Two days a week she visits children in hospitals. The kids there are often very ill. Some have a disease and have to stay for a long time. Others have had an operation. Magic stops by to make them feel better. She helps them to forget about the doctors and needles and wherever it hurts, and reminds them to smile for a while.

You might be surprised to see a horse inside a hospital. Magic, however, is not a large horse. She is a miniature horse, about the size of a German shepherd dog. The first thing you notice about Magic is her beautiful, light blue eyes. She has black hair and a white patch on her face. Every day before going to the hospital, Magic gets a bath and has her hair brushed. She wears a special blue and gold coat to let everyone know she's working.

Magic seems to know who needs her most. When she walks into a room, she goes right up to one of the children. Sometimes she puts her head in their lap. Sometimes she presses her forehead against theirs. Other times she stands very close. She's gone through years of training to learn how to do what her handler asks. But most of what she does comes naturally. She just wants to make the boys and girls feel better.

Being in a hospital can be frightening for children. There are strange tests, weird noises, and scary new equipment. Some kids have to get around in a wheelchair. Magic tries to make it fun for them. She trots beside their

Magic the caring miniature horse

wheelchair around the hospital halls. *Clip clop,* her hooves tap on the tiles. Magic has no trouble walking on slippery hospital floors. She can even go up and down the stairs and ride in the elevator.

One time, a very sick little girl got to make a wish. She wished to have a tea party with Magic. Magic got all dressed up in a special cape with silver sparkles and a red bow. She even wore a black hat with fancy feathers. Magic and her handler walked into the hospital room. The girl was there waiting with ribbons in her hair and a huge smile. A table was set with tea cups, saucers, and yummy treats. Magic was the perfect guest. "This is my best day ever," the girl said.

After every visit, Magic's handler leads her back to the trailer. First there is work, then play. "Magic, shake it off," he says. Magic has fun prancing and romping before going home.

Magic lives with a herd of other horses on a large ranch. When she gets out of the trailer, her horse pals Dream and Sweetheart trot over to greet her. Then, they all go off to play together. Magic loves to run and jump with her friends, and eat grass in the field. Magic's handler makes her life as natural as possible, like a horse in the wild. The horses in the herd have acres of land to move about in all day.

Magic

BREED: American Miniature Horse

AGE: 10 years

COLOR: black

WEIGHT: 100 lbs.

FAVORITE FOOD: grass

FAVORITE TOY: soccer ball

LIVES IN: Florida

In addition to visiting hospitals, Magic goes to libraries and classrooms. She listens to stories that school kids read to her. Her handler calls her reading program *Reading is Magic*. Wouldn't it seem like magic to read a book to a horse?

Sometimes Magic has a very difficult job to do. She and other miniature horses travel all across the country to help those in great need. In one case, families lost their homes to a hurricane. Other times, whole towns were damaged in an earthquake, fire, or flood. If there is a tragedy, Magic and her handler set off to help. When children are going through something terrible, Magic brings them comfort and hope. For that, she's won many awards, including The Most Heroic Pet in America. After a difficult visit, her handler reminds her, "Shake it off, Magic."

Even though she's famous, Magic is always the happiest when she's helping others.

I was very worried
and upset, but you comforted
me and made me happy!
—Psalm 94:19

5
Ricochet

Ricochet runs into the waves and splashes, chasing a gull that glides through the salty air. She's as comfortable in the ocean as a fish or a seal. In California, almost everyone likes to go to the beach. Even dogs.

She stops beside a long, striped surfboard in the sand. A slim boy sits beside it, waiting. He wears a shiny, black wet suit and a life vest. He has some physical challenges. Some things that are easy for most children are not easy for him. He's never played many sports. He isn't sure about surfing. But Ricochet knows all about surfing. Ricochet gives him a kiss. *You can do it!* She noses her own pink life vest. The two are going to have a fun adventure together.

It all began in a little wading pool in Ricochet's yard. At the time, the golden retriever pup was only a few months old. She'd been in training to be a therapy dog. Her mom, Judy, taught her how to sit, stay, how to retrieve objects, open doors, and turn on lights. Ricochet is smart. Judy put a small surfboard in the wading pool. Ricochet climbed right on. She could balance on the surfboard.

Ricochet likes surfing as much as a duck likes swimming. One day Ricochet was surfing in the ocean next to a teenager named Patrick. Patrick had a physical disability and wasn't able to use his arms or legs. But he wanted to surf, so he was lying down on the board in the water. All of a sudden, Ricochet jumped off her own surfboard and right onto the surfboard with Patrick. She shifted her weight to balance the board in the waves, something Patrick couldn't do by himself. "It's like they've been surfing together forever," Judy said.

Why did Ricochet jump on the surfboard that day? Because helping others feel the joy of surfing is her purpose. Since then, Ricochet has surfed with hundreds of kids and adults. She helps people with disabilities, people in wheelchairs, and people who have different needs.

Ricochet the surfing dog

Ricochet

BREED: Golden Retriever

AGE: 10 years

COLOR: red

WEIGHT: 60 lbs.

FAVORITE FOOD: chicken

FAVORITE TOY: ball that laughs when played with

LIVES IN: California

So now it is the young boy's turn. Adults help him onto the surfboard and tow him out into the water. Ricochet jumps on the board. The boy holds onto Ricochet's life vest. At first he is afraid he might fall off. But Ricochet knows what she's doing. She's done this plenty of times before. She helps the boy feel safe. He throws back his head and laughs. They're surfing!

Ricochet was never taught how to surf with children with different needs. She just knows what to do. Every child has certain abilities and certain weaknesses. Ricochet allows each child to use their abilities, and at the same time she helps them with what they need. Because of her extraordinary gifts, Surf Dog Ricochet has earned many awards. She's received the *AKC award for Canine Excellence*, and the *American Humane Association's Hero Dog Award*. And she is in two *Surf Dog Hall of Fames*.

Be all you can be. That's what Ricochet seems to say. Ricochet has another message she wants to share with young people. Because she's a gentle dog, sometimes other dogs push her around. If there are bigger, stronger dogs on the beach, Ricochet always ends up on the bottom of the pile. She never fights back. We should treat others the way we want to be treated. And no one likes getting pushed and shoved. "No one should be a bully," Judy says, "and no one should get bullied." Sometimes she and Ricochet visit schools and talk about bullying. When the students think about such a sweet, gentle dog being bullied, they understand. They don't want Ricochet to be hurt. And if it's wrong for dogs, it's also wrong for people. Maybe they wouldn't have thought of that if Judy and Ricochet hadn't shared their story.

At the end of every day, even for such a busy dog, there is always time for fun. Ricochet loves to play with balls, and carries them everywhere. She loves her little sister—a yellow lab-golden retriever mix named Cori. And she loves chasing gulls on the beach—but she always lets them get away.

My brother, you have shown
love to God's people,
and your help has greatly
encouraged them.
—PHILEMON 1:7

6

Bacon Bits

"Do you like my dog?" a friendly woman named Terry asks as she enters a classroom.

The kids run over to see the chubby animal that Terry has on a leash. A girl with freckles notices the animal's wide nose and curly tail. "That's a pig," she says.

Terry looks surprised and pretends to gasp. "You just called my dog a pig!" All the kids burst into laughter. "This is Bacon Bits," Terry announces, "and yes, you're right, he is a pig." Bacon Bits grunts, as if to say "You bet I am."

Bacon Bits is a pot-bellied pig, and he's about the size of a Golden Retriever. Three bands of different colors wrap across his body—first a stripe of gold, then a stripe of pink, then a stripe of white. His skin is covered in coarse bristles, like what you'd find on a hair brush, or on a stiff brush your parents might use to clean a floor or polish shoes. He trots—very slowly—on short legs with little hooves. He looks like he's walking on tippy-toe.

Bacon Bits has a special purpose. He's a therapy pig, and he has the busiest schedule of any pig you ever knew. He goes visiting almost every day. He stops by schools, camps, libraries, hospitals, airports, parks, church picnics, after-care facilities, vacation Bible school, sporting events, and many other places. He also checks in on adults and seniors in nursing homes and care facilities. Everyone wants Bacon Bits to visit. He's a popular pig! The reason he is so busy is simple—he loves making people happy. And how does he do that? Just by being himself.

"Do you have any questions today?" Terry asks. All the hands in the class shoot up. "How much does he weigh?" they want to know. This is almost always the first question.

"He weighs 125 pounds," Terry answers.

"Where does he live?" a boy asks.

"Bacon Bits lives in the house with us. Do you have a pet dog or cat? They stay in the house with you, right? Well,

Bacon Bits the friendly pot-bellied pig

Bacon Bits is like that. He even waits at the door when he has to go out, just like a dog. And he likes to sleep on the couch."

"Does he eat bacon?" someone else asks.

Terry gets that question a lot. "No, he eats grain. He also gets a pound of carrots, pumpkin, and apples every day. He loves strawberries. And for a treat, we might give him a peppermint patty. And after he eats, guess what? We brush his teeth." At first it sounds funny, but then everyone agrees that brushing your teeth is important.

Bacon Bits also gets a bath every day with special shampoo and conditioner. Terry takes him to a do-it-yourself dog bath. People always laugh to see a pig at the dog bath.

Terry tosses a big red ball onto the floor. Bacon Bits follows it around, pushing it with his nose. It looks like he's trying out for a funny soccer team. He can make little grunting noises, barking sounds, and snorts. He also can make a sound like a cat purring, and a loud squeal when he's upset. Right now, he is happy, so he is grunting: *oink, oink, oink.*

The kids take turns patting Bacon Bits. "I've never seen a real pig before," one boy says. Terry tells them that pigs are smart and friendly, just like a dog. They are caring and

Bacon Bits

BREED: Pot-Bellied Pig

AGE: 2 years

COLOR: pink and gold and white

WEIGHT: 125 lbs.

FAVORITE FOOD: strawberries

FAVORITE TOY: ball

LIVES IN: New York

loving animals. The kids promise to treat all animals with kindness.

The teacher says, "We read a book about a pig—it's called *Charlotte's Web.*"

"That is one of our favorite books," Terry says. "Maybe we can read it to Bacon Bits. Would anyone like to take a turn?"

The freckled girl takes the book off the shelf. She sits beside Bacon Bits and puts an arm around his warm, bristly neck. She starts the story about a spider named Charlotte, and a lonely pig named Wilbur and how he became known as Some Pig .

Whoever has the gift
of showing kindness to others
should do it gladly.
—ROMANS 12:8

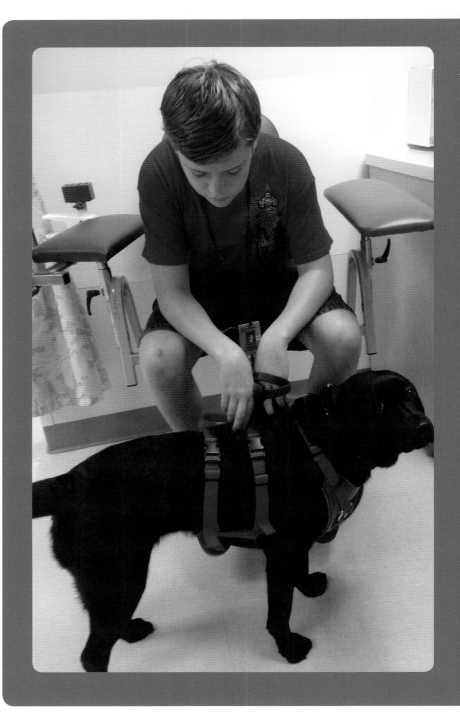

7
Parfait

Joseph and his parents get ready to go to church. They all pile into the SUV—everyone, including a big, black dog. Parfait goes almost everywhere with them—even to church. They all walk into the worship center together. As the pastor speaks, the dog lies on the floor in front of the pews. Some people joke that the sermon puts her to sleep. The music plays and everyone sings. Good thing Parfait doesn't howl.

On the way home in the car, Parfait lifts her shiny black nose in the air. Joseph's mom calls it *air sniffing*. Why is sniffing the air important? Parfait is Joseph's service dog. She can tell, by a scent, when Joseph needs help. On the way home, Joseph suddenly stares straight ahead. He looks okay, but Parfait knows better. *Woof, woof*, she barks, loud and deep.

Joseph is having a seizure. His father pulls over. "Good girl, Parfait," his mother says.

A seizure is when the brain doesn't work right. When a seizure happens, one moment Joseph is fine, and the next moment he seems far away. He isn't in pain, but for a while he is not aware of what is happening around him. An adult is needed to make sure he's okay.

Joseph does not know when he is about to have a seizure. But Parfait does. When the brain starts acting up, the body creates a certain scent. Parfait has been trained to detect this scent. No human can smell this. But a dog's nose is thousands of times more sensitive than a human's nose. And, Parfait has never been wrong.

The seizure lasts only a few minutes. It may look scary, but when it's over, Joseph is fine. He hugs Parfait. "You're my best friend," he says. Her wagging tail shows that she feels the same way. She leans in close. She will always do anything she can for her boy.

Joseph also has a disorder called autism. This makes it hard for him to deal with the world around him. Parfait helps him feel more comfortable in public. People sometimes come up to him and ask him about his dog. He doesn't like talking much, but he will always speak up about his dog. And sharing about Parfait is a good way to make new friends.

One of Joseph's favorite activities is swimming. He's a member of a swim team. Of course, Parfait goes along to the pool. She's a Labrador retriever, a breed of dog that

Parfait the seizure alert dog

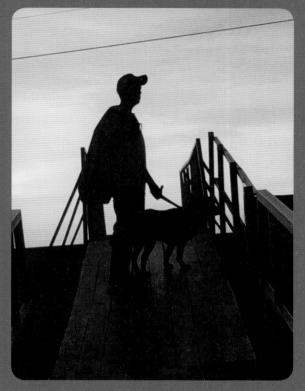

loves the water. Her fur is thick and smooth. Her legs are short and strong, making her an excellent swimmer. Her broad tail can steer her like a boat's rudder. She would enjoy taking a few laps around the pool, but she doesn't jump in. She sits on a bench with Joseph's mom and watches her boy. She always pays attention when she's working.

When Parfait senses Joseph's seizure, she gives what Joseph's mom calls her *big girl bark*. Parfait won't stop barking until someone responds. Parfait has never sounded her big girl bark when Joseph is in the water. This is because the strong-smelling chemicals used in swimming pools make it difficult for Parfait to smell anything else. But she is still there for her very best friend.

One place Parfait doesn't go is to school. A child with autism is not allowed to manage his service dog without an adult handler. The teachers and others are trained to aid Joseph if he has a seizure during school. So Parfait waits by the window for Joseph to come home. She's so happy when her best friend returns. Then they go outside in the big yard and play fetch. Joseph and Parfait are lucky because they have each other.

Parfait

BREED: Labrador Retriever

AGE: 5 years

COLOR: black

WEIGHT: 60 lbs.

FAVORITE FOOD: pepperoni-flavored dog treats

FAVORITE TOY: hard plastic chew-bone

LIVES IN: Missouri

You can go to him for protection. . . . You can trust him to surround and protect you like a shield.
—PSALM 91:4

8
Tess

A woman walks into a large, comfortable living room. She's carrying an animal snuggled in a soft, sturdy cushion. The animal is about the size of a football. Some kids who are staying at the house come closer to see. The animal peeks out of the blanket. A twitchy nose pokes out. Brown fur. And two long floppy ears.

Tess the therapy bunny has come to visit the Ronald McDonald House. It's not a place to get hamburgers and French fries. And it's not a house where just one family lives together, either. Different families stay there for a short time when they have a child who is in the hospital. Sometimes, kids have to go to a hospital that is not close to their own home. When you are sick, having your family nearby is as helpful as medicine. This house provides a place for mothers, fathers, sisters, and brothers to stay together close to a hospital. Maybe it's a little bit like it was for Tess the rabbit. She used to live in a shelter. It wasn't her real home, either. Now she lives in a comfortable "condo" at the Bunnies in Baskets studio in Portland, Oregon.

The woman named Sarah asks the kids if they'd like to visit with Tess. A shy girl gets comfortable on a chair, and Sarah covers her lap with Tess's special blanket. The name Tess is embroidered in the corner. Then she places the soft rabbit on the girl's lap. Tess loves to be held. She's very calm and doesn't wiggle. Sometimes she looks at the person who is holding her. Sometimes she just hangs out. The girl has been thinking about her brother in the hospital. She doesn't tell her mom and dad how she feels. They are worried too. She doesn't want to make them feel any worse. So she's kept it to herself. But she can tell Tess.

"Tess is a good listener," Sarah says.

"She must be, because she has such big ears," the girl says. She whispers into Tess's ear. Tess will never tell anyone her secrets.

When she's not visiting, Tess hops around her condo and exercises on the floor of Bunnies in Baskets. Rabbits

Tess

BREED: Mixed-breed rabbit

AGE: 2 years

COLOR: brown, white

WEIGHT: 8 lbs.

FAVORITE FOOD: parsley

FAVORITE TOY: puzzles with treats hidden in them

LIVES IN: Oregon

I will change their sadness into happiness. I will comfort my people, making them happy instead of sad.

—JEREMIAH 31:13

need a lot of room to be happy and healthy. She can hop around the studio and uses the litter box like a cat. She also likes the company of other rabbits at Bunnies in Baskets. She plays with her brother, Pansy. Tess is very active, curious, and playful. She has balls to toss, tunnels to crawl through, and toys that reward her with treats.

Another day Pansy joins Tess on a visit. Two new boys hold the rabbits. They don't know each other very well, and it feels awkward. At first, they don't say much. One boy holds Tess and pets her soft fur. Tess senses that her boy needs her to be close. She snuggles up under his chin. He holds her gently. For a long time, he is silent. There has been a lot of talk lately about hospitals and treatments. He wonders if it's okay to think about anything else. Thinking about hospitals all the time is difficult.

"Where do you go to school?" he asks quietly.

The other boy answers. "Do you play a sport?" he adds.

Before long they are sharing things that all other kids discuss. School. Music. Friends. Tess cuddles in as the boy talks. One ear droops. This happens when she is relaxed. Because the boy has loosened up, Tess is calm and comfortable, too. The boy laughs. For the first time in a long time, he thinks about something other than being sick or worried. It feels good to relax, just like Tess.

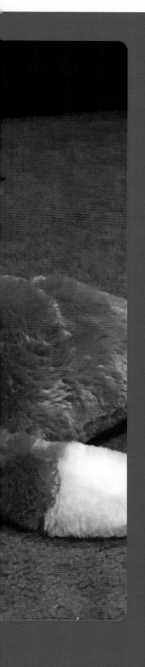

9
Lentil

A white French bulldog with peanut butter-brown patches wiggles in a little boy's arms. "He looks just like me," the boy says.

A boy and a dog—how could they look alike? The dog's ears don't look like the boy's ears. The dog's ears are rounded and stick up like two pompoms on top of a hat.

Their noses don't look the same. The dog's nose is shiny and shaped like a heart.

But the dog's mouth? Well, you might say his smile is crooked. There is a gap above his teeth, and some of his gums show. The boy's mouth looks like that, too. He was born with a condition called cleft palate. The dog has cleft palate too. The boy is excited to see a dog with the same smile.

The dog's name is Lentil. A lentil is a kind of a bean. When Lentil was born he was so small he looked almost like a bean. Right from the start, though, something was different. His mouth did not form properly. It looks different from other dogs' mouths. He also had trouble eating. Water dripped down his chin and all over the floor. He made funny snorts when he breathed. So Lentil had to have an operation. It helped him eat and breathe better. But his mouth will always look a little different.

Lentil lives in a home with his human mom, dad, a little girl, a cute black dog, and a hairless cat. They all get along together. His human mom is a woman named Lindsay. She takes care of Lentil and makes sure he is happy. And Lentil is very happy. He likes to chew a soft toy named Stinky and chase his dirty yellow tennis ball. He sniffs around the grassy yard with his friends. He takes naps on the couch. Lentil does everything other dogs do.

He can also do something special. He teaches children to accept their differences. Lindsay takes Lentil to visit schools, camps, and hospitals. Most of the kids Lentil visits have cleft palate. Lentil snuggles with them and gives them kisses. He is so happy to be with them that he wiggles all over and wags his stubby tail.

Lentil the cleft palate dog

Lentil

BREED: French Bulldog

AGE: 5 years

COLOR: fawn and white

WEIGHT: 20 lbs.

FAVORITE FOOD: seafood

FAVORITE TOY: tennis ball

LIVES IN: New Jersey

I praise you
because you made me
in such a wonderful way.
—PSALM 139:14

The children love and accept Lentil just the way he is. When they see this adorable dog who is a little different, they feel it is okay to be a little different, too.

When Lentil goes to work, he rides in the car in a special seat. It looks like a soft, lined basket, attached with buckles. Lentil is always safe.

There is always plenty of time for fun. In the summer he wades in a shallow inflatable pool. In the fall, he plays with Stinky in a pile of leaves. Lentil likes to help Lindsay in the garden, making sure the watermelon and pumpkins are growing just right. When no one is looking, he digs in the dirt. He can't help getting into a little mischief once in a while! Once, he found a yellow rubber ducky toy. But it wasn't a toy for dogs. He didn't mean to be bad, it just seemed fun to chew on. When asked, he gave it back. He only put a few holes in it.

Most summers, Lindsay and Lentil spend a week at a special camp for kids with cleft palate. This is one of the best weeks of their whole summer. They join in with games, hikes, and arts and crafts. There's even a campfire in the evenings with roasted marshmallows. Do you think Lentil is the best dog-camper around? He helps kids see that everyone should smile. Because no matter how it looks, a smile is always beautiful.

10
Oliver

Dust kicks up as Oliver trots around the horse ring. Long, white hair on his feet flutters as he moves. It looks as if he's wearing boots, but the white hairs are called feathers. A girl in leggings and a riding helmet sits on his back. He senses that the girl is nervous. He slows a little and bobs his head. *I've got you*, he seems to say. *No worries.*

Oliver is a draft horse. We usually think of draft horses as huge animals. But Oliver is short. Horses are measured in "hands." Oliver is just over fourteen hands. That is about five feet tall at his shoulder. This makes him the perfect size to work with kids. He's strong enough to carry them, but not so big as to be scary. Oliver has a special job to do. He helps children with different abilities. He is very gentle, and he seems to know who is on his back and what they need.

One day, a girl arrives to see Oliver. She has cerebral palsy (also called CP). She cannot walk, talk, or play the way most children her age do. So, she gets special help called physical therapy. When Oliver is involved, it is called Physical Therapy on Horseback. The act of riding Oliver helps strengthen the girl's muscles. This is because when a person sits on a horse, they use the same joints and muscles as they do when walking. Oliver nickers softly and starts moving. A man holds a rope and leads Oliver. A woman walks beside the girl to keep her from falling. Oliver knows just what to do. He keeps a steady and careful pace.

Later, a different girl performs exercises on top of Oliver. Yes, exercise on top of a horse! The man and the woman help. The girl stands tall and straight on a blanket over Oliver's back. She kneels. She lifts one leg. The exercises help her practice balance. Eventually she may be able to stand or kneel on Oliver while he is moving around the ring.

Oliver's handlers take care of him, brush him, and give him food and water. He leans into them for a cuddle. He nudges them so they won't stop. There is always time for loving.

Oliver the gentle draft horse

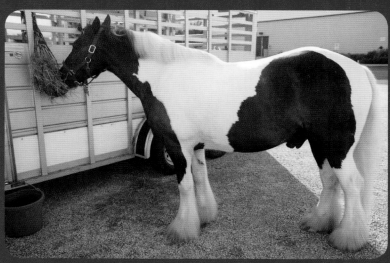

Oliver

BREED: Gypsy Vanner

AGE: 10 years

COLOR: white with black spots

WEIGHT: 1200 lbs.

FAVORITE FOOD: grass

FAVORITE PLAYMATE: Halfinger pony
named Gabe

LIVES IN: Missouri

Another day, a sandy-haired boy runs up to the rail. He has autism. He doesn't always understand other people. Other people don't always understand him. Oliver is part of his therapy. The boy climbs into the saddle. An instructor tells him to turn left. The boy kicks his feet and points to the left. Oliver looks back at him. *What do you want me to do?* he seems to say. "Oliver doesn't understand you," the instructor says. "How does that make you feel?"

"Angry," the boy says.

The instructor guides the boy to make a connection between how he feels and how Oliver must feel when they don't understand things. He teaches the boy how to show the horse what he wants him to do. "You squeeze the rein like this," the instructor says. The boy tries it. Oliver turns left. A wide grin spreads across the boy's face. "We did it!"

Oliver likes to work, but most of the time he's just like any other horse. He lives in a pasture and munches on grass. Even on chilly days, he plays outside. He doesn't need a blanket. His hair is so thick and heavy it keeps him warm. He sleeps outside, except on very cold or rainy nights. Then he sleeps inside in a dry, warm stall. No one likes to sleep outside in the rain.

He loves carrots and apples for treats. Sometimes his handler holds out a closed hand. Inside is a special treat.

A peppermint. One Easter the kids were having an egg hunt. Candy eggs were hidden all over. Oliver was curious. He decided to hunt for eggs too. When he found them, he ate them—foil wrapper and all. Oliver also enjoys playing games. Once he saw kids tossing beanbags onto a giant tic-tac-toe board. He had to find a way to join in. He trotted over, picked up a beanbag in his teeth and tossed it in the air. He didn't get three in a row, but he had fun!

Before long, a pony named Gabe trots up to him. They touch noses. It looks as if they are talking. They gallop off together to play in the pasture. After a day of work, there is nothing better than relaxing with your best buddy.

He will make you strong.
He will support you
and keep you from falling.
—1 PETER 5:10

11
Murfy

Murfy pads around the *Arrivals and Departures* sign at the airport. He's a big dog, with thick brown fur and huge white feet. People usually notice him. But this time they all stare at the sign. Bold yellow letters blink. *Flight delayed. Flight canceled.* Murfy looks at the passengers waiting in lines. Good thing he's at the airport today. People are going to need him.

There is bad weather out west. Thunderstorms have stopped planes from taking off. It's not safe for them to travel during bad weather. But that doesn't help the people waiting to take a trip. They all have someplace to go. Having to change travel plans can be difficult.

Murfy is a therapy dog at the Albany International Airport. He and his handler, Katrina, visit the airport to help travelers feel less anxious. They have received clearance to walk through the TSA checkpoint and other public areas. Sometimes a child is afraid to get on a plane. Or security looks scary. Sometimes people are just tired and irritable after a busy day. Murfy looks around. He has a knack for finding people who need him. When someone is upset, he takes their mind off their worries and makes them feel better.

Murfy sees a family at one of the gate waiting areas. He tugs Katrina toward the family. Murfy senses this family is upset and needs some help. Katrina learns that their flight has been canceled due to the bad weather. The father talks to an airline agent. "Can you get us home to Chicago?" he asks. The mother chases after her young twins. "Don't run. Don't climb on the chairs. Please behave." The little boys are tired of behaving. They are only two years old, and they don't understand about the delay. The mother pushes her hair out of her face and sighs. She wants to sit down and relax.

Luckily, here comes Murfy. He walks right up to the boys. Their eyes grow wide. "Big doggy!" they say.

"This is Murfy," Katrina says. "Would you like to play with him?"

Murfy the airport dog

The boys run up and hug Murfy. They bury their faces in his thick brown fur. He smells and feels nice. Murfy gets a bath and a brushing before visits. Katrina wants everyone who meets him to remember his soft, beautiful, well-groomed coat. Murfy lies down and the boys pat and rub him all over. They especially love his big, bushy tail. Before long, they've unpacked their travel bag and have shown Murfy all their toys. "Read books," they say. They open the pages and show Murfy the pictures. Murfy lets them crawl all around him. Newfoundlands are a strong, working breed of dog. Murfy is even trained to pull a cart in the summer and a sled in the winter. So the busy boys don't upset him at all. The kids march their plastic figures on top of him. They move the toys up the dog's side like a mountain. Murfy tries hard not to wiggle so the toys won't fall.

The mother finally sits and rests. At last the twins grow tired. They lie on the floor beside the big dog and kiss him. He kisses them back with his wet tongue. The boys giggle.

"Murfy saved the day," their mother says. Murfy gets up and gives her a big, sloppy kiss too!

Murfy seems to sense the needs not only of people, but of animals too. Good thing, because he lives with three other dogs, four cats, two turtles, and three rabbits. Katrina is a licensed New York State Wildlife Rehabber. She takes

Murfy

BREED: Newfoundland

AGE: 4 years

COLOR: brown with white markings

WEIGHT: 145 lbs.

FAVORITE FOOD: ice cream

FAVORITE TOY: cupcake squeaky toy

LIVES IN: New York

care of orphaned and injured wildlife. Sometimes Murfy shares his home with squirrels, bunnies, and birds. Murfy loves them all.

At last it is time to go for the day. They head toward the door, but Murfy pulls at his leash. He stares straight ahead. There is a woman and a young girl at the ticket desk. The girl plops down to the floor and pouts. Murfy walks toward her. It looks as if Murfy is ready to help someone else who needs him. Murfy always knows.

Come to me all of you who are
tired from the heavy burden
you have been forced to carry.
I will give you rest.
—MATTHEW 11:28

12
Sheldon
& Spencer

It's exam time at school. The students walk around with piles of books and papers. They're anxious and tired after studying hard. When they walk down the hall, what do they see? A woman seated at a table with two small animals, wrapped in blankets. "We're here to give stress relief," the woman, Shannon, says. "Would you like to visit with us?"

The kids gather around and check out the cuddly critters. One animal sticks his little nose out of the blanket. His bright, round eyes peer up curiously. "This is Sheldon, and the other one is Spencer. They're guinea pigs."

One girl asks to hold Sheldon. She cradles him like a baby. "Look," she says. "Baby pigs!"

"Actually, they are full grown. And they're not pigs at all," Shannon says. "They're rodents. And another strange fact—they're not from Guinea. They're originally from South America." Everyone is surprised to learn this.

Sheldon and Spencer are therapy animals. They love to be held, and don't bite, wiggle, or try to run away. Guinea pigs make great therapy animals because they are small and quiet. Some people are afraid of more common therapy animals, such as dogs. Kids can get up close to Sheldon and Spencer. They can hold them and feed them lettuce and parsley. Usually, you don't get to feed therapy dogs.

A boy with a heavy backpack walks out of a classroom. He has a test the next period. He's worried that he won't do well. He sees the guinea pigs' cute faces and chubby bodies and joins the other students. He strokes the white fur on Spencer's nose. When he pulls aside the blanket, his eyes grow wide. The rest of Spencer is bald. "Why did you cut his hair?" he asks.

"I didn't. Sheldon and Spencer are a breed of hairless guinea pig called Skinny Pig," Shannon says.

"Really? But why?"

Sheldon & Spencer
the hairless guinea pigs

Sheldon

BREED: Skinny Pig

AGE: 4 years

COLOR: brown

WEIGHT: 2 lbs.

FAVORITE FOOD: cherry tomatoes

FAVORITE TOY: wooden edible balls

LIVES IN: Ontario, Canada

Spencer

BREED: Skinny Pig

AGE: 3 years

COLOR: brown with white nose

WEIGHT: 3 lbs.

FAVORITE FOOD: corn husks

FAVORITE TOY: cardboard tube

LIVES IN: Ontario, Canada

"It's the same reason some people have blue eyes and some have brown eyes. Some have blond hair and some have red hair. Guinea pigs come in all different colors and combinations of colors—white, brown, cream, golden, black, silver—and all different hair lengths. Some have short hair and some have very long, flowing hair. And some, like Sheldon and Spencer, have practically no hair."

Even though the Skinny Pigs are mostly hairless, they still need to be groomed. Before visits, they have baths and get their nails trimmed. Shannon rubs coconut oil in their skin. This keeps them healthy, plus they look clean and neat for pictures. "Can we take selfies with them?" the students ask. The Skinny Pigs are used to having their pictures taken. Shannon likes to photograph them eating veggies and dressing up for holidays.

Sheldon and Spencer stay very still when they're working. But at home, they get to run around as much as they want. They don't stay in a cage. During the day, they roam loose in the house. Sometimes they go outside for fresh air. Sheldon and Spencer keep to the shade. If not, they could get sunburned. They love playing with their pal—a sweet Chocolate Lab named Sasha. Sasha keeps watch over them. She barks if they get into mischief. The three of them curl up and snooze together in front of the fireplace. When they are bored, Sheldon and Spencer might nibble on Sasha's tail. *Ouch!* Sometimes, best friends have to be forgiving.

If the kids are lucky, they will hear some of the different noises guinea pigs make. Sometimes they grunt or snort. They can make a sound like a whistle. They purr when they're content. *Wheek, wheek, wheek!* Spencer makes a squeaky noise. "I think he's hungry. Would you like to feed him?" Shannon asks.

"Will he bite?" the boy asks.

Shannon shakes her head and gives the boy a long, slender piece of parsley. He holds it for Spencer to munch. Soon Spencer wants another. And another. "He sure can eat a lot," the boy says. After a while he realizes it's time for his test. He feels much more relaxed.

"I was having a bad day. I was all worried," he says, patting Sheldon and Spencer one more time.

"But now it's okay."

You cannot add
any time to your life
by worrying about it.
—MATTHEW 6:27

13
Monty

Monty stretches his shaggy black paws and yawns. It's time for school. He hurries into the kitchen and gobbles his breakfast. Someone helps him into his red and black vest. He's ready to go. But not to *dog* school. He goes to a regular middle school with his girl, Faith. Monty is Faith's service dog.

When she was born, some of the bones in Faith's legs didn't grow right. Because of this, she is shorter than other kids her age. She uses crutches to walk. But she goes to school, takes piano lessons, and hangs out with her friends just like any other girl. She has a problem with her legs, but everything else is okay.

Faith gets ready for school, too. When she reaches down to get her shoe, she says, "Monty, brace." This is Monty's command to stand still and firm. Faith leans her arms across his back and pulls herself up. Before, she would have needed to ask her mom or dad for help. Monty is a Mobility Assistance Dog. *Mobility* means the ability to move around freely and easily. Monty helps her get around and do more things for herself.

When Monty was a puppy in Alabama, tornadoes destroyed his home. He was rescued by a group that trains shelter dogs to be service dogs. He came to live with Faith when she was in the fourth grade. Faith had to take special classes to learn how to work with Monty. Both she and Monty had a lot to learn. "He's very stubborn," Faith said.

Her mom laughed. "Sometimes you can be stubborn too. You two should do well together."

In school, Monty is everyone's friend. "Hi, Monty!" the other students call. But they've learned that they can't touch or pat him when he's working. When a service dog is on the job, they shouldn't be distracted.

In Faith's first class, Monty tries to lie under the desk, but his big head sticks out into the aisle. His tail sticks out on the other side. "He's trained to stay under tables so he

Monty the mobility support dog

Monty

BREED: Lab mix

AGE: 5 years

COLOR: black

WEIGHT: 82 lbs.

FAVORITE FOOD: bacon

FAVORITE TOY: sock monkey

LIVES IN: Illinois

won't be in the way," Faith explains. But some of the middle school desks aren't big enough for Monty.

After class, Monty walks beside Faith down the hall to her locker. He has a backpack with two pockets that hang over his vest. Faith slips a folder into his backpack. A paperback book falls out of the locker. "Monty, take it," she says. Monty picks up the book in his mouth and takes it to her. She slides the paperback book into his backpack too.

Her next class is upstairs. Climbing stairs is difficult for Faith. She hangs onto a handle on Monty's vest. Because he is big and strong, he can help support Faith as she climbs up the stairs. At the end of the hall there is a heavy door. Monty jumps up and hits the handicap button next to the door. Faith can go right through. Monty can turn on light switches, too.

Monty attends after school activities with Faith. He goes to orchestra practice, and hangs out in the dugout with her during Miracle League softball games. He loves to play. But he won't run and chase the balls when he's working. One time he went to Boston with the family. "We're going to take the Duck Tour," Faith told him. They climbed into a big car with rows of seats. Monty seemed fine as they drove around the streets. Then they plunged into the river. The Duck Tour vehicle is made to travel on land and water. Was Monty ever surprised!

As Faith gets older, she wants to do more things on her own. She enjoys activities apart from her family. She doesn't like always having to ask her friends to help. Now that she has Monty, she doesn't need to rely on other people as much. She can always depend on faithful Monty. And Monty can always depend on Faith.

*I know I was ready to fall,
but, Lord, your faithful love
supported me.*
—PSALM 94:18

14
Sage

Sage arches his long neck over the fence. Some kids are coming down the hill toward the pasture, and he's ready to greet them. Sage is a Bactrian camel, the kind with two humps. He is bigger than a horse, and has shaggy, rusty-brown fur. He has two toes on each foot, and thick, leathery pads on his feet.

Sage lives far away from his natural home in the desert. He and his camel pal Phoenix grew up in the Sacred Camel Gardens of California. From there, they were gifted to a special farm and school outside of New York City. Even though it is not hot and sandy like the desert, they live there very comfortably. They have a lot of company. There are horses, cows, goats, llamas, rabbits, and ducks. There are deer, owls, snakes, and frogs. Plenty of workers take good care of them, and students and teachers visit every day.

This day, a boy with a gray hoodie comes up to the fence and stops to watch Sage. He and his teacher have come from the school. The school is located in a building near the barn and pastures. The boy attends this special school because he has extra challenges. Sometimes he has trouble with his emotions. He feels nervous and worried. In his old school, he had a hard time paying attention in class. He needed more attention and special classes. This school helps him to adjust and succeed. And Sage is part of the reason why.

It's pretty cool to have animals as part of your school. All the animals at the farm have a purpose. The kids help take care of them. But they also learn lessons about their own lives. For instance, Vanilla the goat has a pig for a best friend. So Vanilla teaches the value of accepting those who are different. Brooklyn the sheep was orphaned as a lamb. Brooklyn teaches that not everyone gets to be raised by their parents. A chicken has an injured leg. The chicken teaches that even those with disabilities can succeed.

Sage teaches life lessons too. "Do you think you can get Sage into the barn?" the teacher asks. The boy looks

Sage the school camel

up at Sage. The camel is not an animal he's used to dealing with. How is he going to get such a big, heavy animal into the barn? He listens carefully to the teacher and Sage's handler. He watches Sage to see what the camel might do next. Because he is paying close attention to Sage, he is not thinking about his own problems.

Sage stares hard with big, dark eyes and long lashes. "Is he angry?" the boy asks. It is important to learn what an animal is feeling. Because they don't use words, we have to read their body language.

"No," the handler answers. "He is just curious about you. I think he likes you."

The boy takes the rope attached to Sage's halter and pulls. Sage doesn't budge. "Why isn't he moving?"

"What do you think?" the teacher asks.

The boy studies the situation. "Maybe he doesn't know what I want him to do. Maybe he doesn't know where we are going."

Together, the teacher, handler, and boy discuss how to get Sage into the barn. They explain that Sage is very curious and outgoing. Sometimes he is silly and playful and likes a lot of attention. But sometimes he is unsure of himself and looks to Phoenix for direction. Phoenix acts like an older, wiser brother.

Sage

BREED: Bactrian camel

AGE: 8 years

COLOR: brown

WEIGHT: 1,500 lbs.

FAVORITE FOOD: hay

FAVORITE TOY: doesn't play with toys

LIVES IN: New York

The boy decides that Sage might follow Phoenix. Luckily, Phoenix happily goes along with the boy and the handler into the barn. And sure enough, Sage trots right behind. "We did it!" the boy cheers. If he can learn to care for a big, exotic camel, there is no limit to what he can do.

"I have prepared a room for you to sleep in and a place for your camels."

—GENESIS 24:31

15
Indy

Max is a ten-year-old boy who enjoys Matchbox cars and riding his bike. Max also has autism. Autism affects how the brain works. It makes it difficult for him to understand other people and learn new things. Max's family heard about dogs trained to help boys and girls with autism. After much research and planning, they connected with an organization that helped guide them through the process. Max was matched with a young service dog with long blonde fur, short legs, and a friendly expression.

Indy is the perfect companion for Max. He's calm, gentle, and easy-going. Whenever they go out, Indy wears a bright blue vest with a handle. Max's parents hold the leash. Max holds the handle, and another loop goes around his wrist. Indy stays beside Max. He doesn't bark or tug. He understands that he has a job to do. Sometimes, Max used to wander. Now, if Max tries to pull away, his parents tell Indy, "Stay." Indy will not move. So Max will not walk off.

Indy can go almost anywhere with Max and his parents. They go to movies, birthday parties, malls, and grocery stores together. Before Indy, Max had a difficult time shopping with his family. He'd get confused, and he would sometimes argue or cry. Now Indy takes shopping trips, too. He's trained to sense when Max is becoming overwhelmed. A nudge or a paw on Max's arm helps.

Sometimes Indy feels a *tap, tap, tap* on his shoulder. Max taps when he's anxious. Indy presses in close. *I'm here for you, Max,* Indy seems to say. Before, people used to stare when Max had a meltdown in the store. Now, no one in the store stares. They just see a nice boy with his dog. The family can shop together without a problem.

Indy loves sharing Max's after school activities. Autism can make joining in feel awkward. Just by being near, Indy reminds Max that everything is okay. This helps Max join in even more. Indy stays close beside Mat at track and field meets and Special Olympics practices. He helps Max feel comfortable, safe, and confident.

One time a girl came up to Max and asked if she could pat his dog. Max wasn't sure what to say. Indy gave him a nudge. "Yes," Max answered. "He's very soft. I know because I brush him." Max helps feed, walk, and groom Indy. Max needs Indy. And Indy needs Max, too.

During the week, Max goes to school, but Indy waits at home. Indy can't go to school because Max must have an adult, such as one of his parents, to help handle the dog. Indy misses Max when he's at school. He finds a toy Matchbox car and carries it around in his mouth. It's almost like having part of Max with him. After a while, he plays outside. He loves to roll in the leaves in the fall, or run through the snow in the winter. Later, he rests with his head on a nice, soft pillow. He likes a blanket too. Finally, Max comes home. Indy runs up to the door. His tail wags wildly. He gives one joyful bark. When Max comes through the door, Indy does a happy dance.

The first thing Max wants to do after school is be with his dog. He sits next to him on the floor and tells him about his day. Indy listens. They are a team. Partners. Friends.

Nighttime comes. Indy snuggles on the bed beside Max. *It's okay, buddy. I'm here.* Max's Mom offers a bedtime prayer. "Dear Jesus, Thank you for Max and Indy.

Indy

BREED: Golden Retriever

AGE: 4 years

COLOR: light blond

WEIGHT: 70 lbs.

FAVORITE FOOD: tiny dog biscuits

FAVORITE TOY: yellow plastic chew toy with knobby ends

LIVES IN: Michigan

Keep them both safe from harm and danger, accident and illness. Be with everyone who they love and everyone who loves them. Thank you for the blessings of today and the gift of tomorrow. Amen." Feeling safe and warm, both dog and boy drift off to sleep.

The Lord is your Protector.
The Lord stands by your side,
shading and protecting you.

—Psalm 121:5

16
Raul

Raul is the color of a toasted marshmallow. He's soft and fluffy, and just as sweet. He's a beautiful Birman cat, also called the Sacred Cat of Burma.

Raul lives with his family and a younger cat named Carl. One day Raul and Carl were playing. Maybe they were playing hide-and-seek, because all of a sudden, Carl was gone. Raul looked for his friend. He looked in the bedroom. The closet door was just barely open. Carl had squeezed through. But he couldn't figure out how to get back out. Poor Carl. Raul couldn't open the door. But he didn't leave his best friend. He sat in front of the closet door and meowed. He meowed louder. His human mom, Sarah, came in and opened the door. Carl ran out. "Good cat, Raul," she said. "You found Carl!" Raul is a good friend.

Raul makes friends every day. He gets to work at a school with Sarah. She helps kids with different needs and their parents. When kids have learning or emotional challenges, the whole family needs extra support. Raul has a big job—he makes everyone feel safe and comfortable. Well, if Raul can handle Carl the cat, he can certainly handle the kids at school.

There is a lot of work to do at the school. Students come in to see Sarah in a meeting room. Sometimes they have big problems. One day a boy sits down by the desk. He is unhappy in school. He's been having trouble at home. But he doesn't know how to talk about it. "Why don't you tell Raul?" Sarah says.

Raul stretches out on the desk atop a pile of papers. He is wearing a blue vest. The tip of his tail twitches softly. He knows what to do. He stays relaxed and still, leans in close, and listens.

"Well, Raul," the boy says, "I threw a notebook and got into trouble." He strokes Raul's velvety fur. He pauses.

Raul listens.

"And at home I argued and I had to go sit in my room." The boy looks down, his eyes watering.

Raul the faithful cat

Raul

BREED: Birman

AGE: 8 years

COLOR: cream and light brown

WEIGHT: 15 lbs.

FAVORITE FOOD: marshmallows

FAVORITE TOY: catnip banana

LIVES IN: Illinois

Raul listens.

"And then my best friend told me I'm dumb."

Raul rubs his head against the boy's hand. Sarah is proud that Raul helped the boy open up and share what was on his mind. Now it is her turn to help. Together, they figure out ways to handle the difficult situations.

Next, a group of students stops by. "Can I help you?" Sarah asks.

"We just want to see Raul," they say. Sarah lets them push Raul down the hall in a stroller. They brush his fur and give him treats.

Finally, one of the girls speaks up. She's having trouble with her math. "Can you show Raul how to do it?" Sarah asks.

The girl takes out her papers and works at the desk. Raul watches. "You multiply these numbers here," she says. "You divide these, here." She tries hard. "Look, I did it! Did I do a good job, Raul?" she asks. Raul purrs. *Yes.*

Sometimes Raul helps kids who have trouble making friends. They don't feel comfortable saying hello and looking others in the eyes. But they like making friends with Raul. Raul doesn't look anyone in the eyes either. It's easy to make friends with Raul.

At home, Raul and Carl watch squirrels from the sliding glass doors. Raul doesn't hiss or yowl. He doesn't try to chase the squirrels. He just wants to be friends. Raul is a friend to everyone.

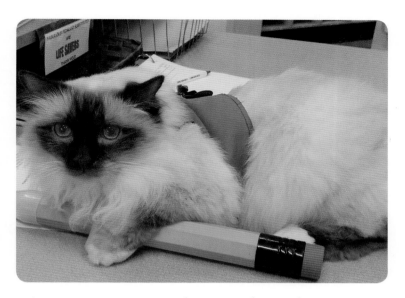

"Friends should be loyal to you
in times of trouble."

—JOB 6:14

17

Molly

Firefighter Dayna walks into the school
room holding the bright red leash of a white dog with
black spots. The room is packed with elementary
school students sitting on the floor. "Ooooh!" they say.
They are excited to see a dog in school. The dog wears
a uniform—a red vest, a plastic firefighter hat, and a
badge. Molly is a real fire dog and a member of Johnson
County RFD #1 in Clarksville, Arkansas.

"Please welcome Molly the Fire Safety Dog," the
principal says.

Molly raises a paw and waves hello. The boys and
girls wave back. They are so excited they can barely
stay seated. Molly shows them her tricks. She can wave,
give high fives, roll over, crawl, and wrap herself up in
a blanket. She knows more than eighty tricks. But her
most important ability is helping to save the lives of
children and their families with her fire safety message.

"Molly is six years old, and she has been in the
fire service since she was a nine-week-old puppy,"

Firefighter Dayna says. Molly is also the mascot of the Keep Kids Fire Safe Foundation. "She is here today to show you what to do in case of a fire."

First, Firefighter Dayna explains about smoke alarms. Smoke alarms make a loud noise when they sense smoke. Then she reads a book about fire safety. Molly helps turn the pages by pushing them with her paw. Dayna sings a fire safety song: "If there is a fire in your house, then your smoke alarm will shout. If there's a fire in your house get out, stay out."

Molly waits to share her important message.

"In a fire, the bad air rises up high." Dayna holds her hand up in the air. "We don't want you to breathe that air. Crawl low under the smoke on your hands and knees. The air down low is cleaner and cooler." Dayna also explains that everyone should know a safe place to meet outside the house.

Molly gets ready. This is her big moment. "We'll use this post as Molly's outside meeting place. Now Molly will show you how to get out of the house and go to her outside meeting place."

Molly stretches forward. "Okay, Molly," Dayna says. Molly crawls low on her belly. The kids laugh and clap. Molly goes to the post. Then she sits and gives Dayna a high five. "That's right Molly," says Dayna. "You crawled

Molly the fire safety dog

low and went to your outside meeting place. Thank you for showing us all what to do if we are ever in a fire." Dayna, or another person, could have demonstrated how to crawl. But a dog is more interesting. The kids remember Molly.

Molly and Dayna have taken their important message all over the world. So far, they've given presentations in 27 states, and they've Skyped with kids in 44 states and 25 different countries. Molly makes the fire safety message interesting and fun. Molly even has coloring pages and activities on her website and Facebook page. Sometimes children send her messages and emails. They thank her for what she has taught them, and they tell her she's a good dog.

Of course, a dog can't think about fire safety all the time. Molly loves to play. Frisbee and fetch are her favorite games. She also plays tag and hide-and-seek with her little Dalmatian brother. Boden is learning to be a fire safety dog too. Molly helps teach him what he needs to know. She shows him her tricks, such as how to crawl low. Then they go outside and play. Molly has a lot of energy, and running around with her brother keeps her fit and healthy.

One of the things Molly loves most is riding on the shiny, red firetrucks when they go to visit schools. She proudly sits right up front, next to the firefighter heroes. And for many kids, Molly is a hero, too.

Molly

BREED: Dalmatian

AGE: 6 years

COLOR: white with black spots

WEIGHT: 55 lbs.

FAVORITE FOOD: sweet potato treats

FAVORITE TOY: purple ball

LIVES IN: Arkansas

Lord, you are my strength
and my protection.
You are a safe place to run to
in time of trouble.
—JEREMIAH 16:19

18
Cloud

Cloud sits in a cute little picnic basket, as still as can be. He's soft as a feather and as white as cotton. He doesn't move one bit.

"Is he real?" a girl with long, black hair asks.

"Yes, he's real," Daleen answers. "His name is Cloud, and he's a ring-necked dove."

Most of the kids have never seen a dove up close. Some have heard of a dove from the story of Noah's Ark. "Can we touch him?" they ask.

Daleen takes Cloud out of his basket and sets him on a blanket on the table. "See how his legs look like little dinosaur legs?" she says. He wears a tiny stretchy vest called a flight suit. Attached to the vest is a little leash. "Cloud might fly away if he's frightened. So I keep hold of his leash."

The dark-haired girl asks to hold him first. "Doves don't perch on fingers like parakeets," Daleen says. She puts Cloud in the girl's cupped hand. The girl pets Cloud gently. He closes his eyes and looks as if he's going to sleep. This means he feels relaxed.

Cloud was hatched at home, so Daleen has cared for and handled him right from the start. When he was just a baby bird, he was very calm and content. He wasn't afraid of dogs. He wasn't even afraid of cats. He was very comfortable around children. Daleen thought he'd make a good therapy bird. A therapy bird is like any other therapy animal. It visits people and provides comfort and love. Daleen and Cloud passed tests to show that Cloud is healthy and friendly. So now Cloud visits kids in schools, libraries, and many other places.

Next it is a tall boy's turn. "May I feed him?" he asks.

Daleen nods and sprinkles some seed in the boy's palm. "See how his eyes are on the sides of his head? You have to hold the seed low, and not right in front of him the way you'd feed a dog." The boy lowers his hand. In his palm are little round white seeds, some brown seeds, and yellow seeds. Cloud pecks lightly, and the boy

Cloud the peaceful dove

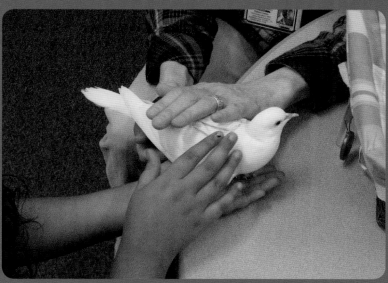

giggles. Cloud eats some of the seed. Then he pushes some onto the floor.

"Why did he do that?"

"Cloud is choosy," Daleen says. "He likes the millet, so he eats that. He doesn't like the cracked corn, so he tosses it away."

"I don't like corn either," the boy says. The others join in, talking about what foods they like and don't like. Children can be picky eaters, just like Cloud.

When the kids have finished visiting, Daleen helps them clean their hands. Then she gives them each a small card. On the front is a picture of Cloud. On the back are some facts about Cloud so they can learn. "We'll never forget Cloud," they say.

After a busy day, Cloud sits back inside the basket to go home. He lives in a big cage in the house. The cage is covered at night, so it will be dark and quiet for sleeping. When Daleen takes the cloth off his cage, he bobs his head and bows. *Coo coo.* This is his way of saying, "Good morning!" His sister Azalea lives in another cage. Some days they fly loose in Daleen's sewing room. When they are loose in the room, she's careful to keep them safe. The family cats might chase the birds. She puts a sign on the door that says, "Birds inside. No cats."

Cloud

BREED: Ring-necked dove

AGE: 9½ years

COLOR: white

WEIGHT: 5½ oz.

FAVORITE FOOD: safflower seed

FAVORITE PLAYMATE: his sister Azalea

LIVES IN: California

This day the California sun is warm and bright. Daleen takes Cloud and Azalea outside to big cages on the covered courtyard. The afternoon is still and quiet. A dove is a symbol of peace, and Cloud looks very peaceful as he rests on a branch.

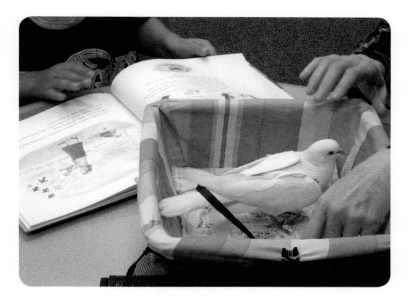

And that afternoon the dove came back to Noah. The dove had a fresh olive leaf in its mouth. This was a sign to show Noah that there was dry ground on the earth.

—Genesis 8:11

19
Oliver & Blue

Most kids like a dog. And many like a cat. Or even a bunny. But a rat?

Some children think rats are bad. They may have read a book about a mean rat. Or seen a movie about a scary rat. But some rats are therapy animals. These special little critters show people that rats are not mean or scary. They can be cute and friendly. Oliver and Blue are two rats that live in different states with different people, but they both do the same things to help kids.

Oliver lives in Georgia with Abby. He is silvery-white and as big as a baked potato. He has round ears, whiskers, and a long pink tail.

Abby takes him to visit kids all over, including Vacation Bible School at churches. At first, the boys and girls aren't sure what to make of him. "Is he a hamster?" "A mouse?" "A ferret?" they ask. Sometimes they're unhappy when Abby says he's a rat. Many kids think rats are dirty. But that isn't true. Before an event, Abby clips Oliver's nails and gives him a nice bath. She scrubs his tail and makes sure he is squeaky clean. Abby wants everyone to know that rats are clean, friendly, and intelligent.

"Does he like cheese?" the kids ask. Abby says he prefers peas, corn, and fruit.

Oliver especially likes to visit during holidays. Holidays are fun, but they can be stressful, too. Everyone is busy. Children are expected to be extra-good. Visiting with a therapy animal such as Oliver can help kids feel more relaxed.

Oliver travels to events in a basket. On holidays, Abby decorates Oliver's basket. At Christmas, it is red with silver jingle bells. On Easter, it looks like an Easter basket, with fake grass and colorful plastic eggs. On St. Patrick's Day, Oliver's basket is green with shamrocks. Abby carries him in the basket, and they march in the St. Patrick's Day parade.

Oliver the friendly rat

One Halloween, Oliver and Abby handed out candy at Trunk or Treat. This is an event like trick or treat, held at her church. Abby dressed up like a character from a Disney movie. She wore a white coat and a tall white chef's hat. There is also a rat in the movie. Oliver didn't even have to wear a costume! "Would you like to meet Oliver?" Abby asked a boy as she tossed some candy in his bag. He frowned because he was blind and couldn't see Oliver. His mother helped him put his hand on the rat. As soon as he felt Oliver, his face lit up with a big, wide grin.

Oliver

BREED: Dumbo Fancy Rat

AGE: 1 ½ years

COLOR: silver

WEIGHT: 1 lb.

FAVORITE FOOD: watermelon

FAVORITE TOY: cardboard box

LIVES IN: Georgia

Blue is another therapy rat. She lives in New York with Barb. Blue is blueish-gray with a white streak on her head, white paws, and a white belly. She is about seven inches long, not counting her long tail. Barb takes Blue to libraries. Her favorite activity is the summer reading program. Dogs, cats, pigs, and other animals read with kids. So why not rats? Blue likes to sit on the library table and listen to kids read books, too.

Barb sometimes carries Blue tucked inside her sweatshirt. Nobody knows she's there. When Barb reaches in and pulls out a rat, some of the kids squeal with surprise. "Let's be very quiet," Barb says. "Can you show me how you move nice and slow?" She explains that rats might get frightened by loud noises and quick movements. She teaches kids how to make Blue comfortable. Sometimes she holds Blue on her lap and the kids gather around. Sometimes the boys and girls sit around a table. Barb places Blue on a towel. Blue is trained not to jump off the table. "You can pat her if you would like," she says.

"I didn't know we could pat a rat," one girl says.

Barb explains that when you see a dog you don't know, you should ask before you pat it. "The same is true for rats. This is my pet and I've given you permission to touch it. If you see a rat running around outside, it is wild and not a pet. Don't touch it." Some kids use two fingers to gently pat Blue. "Her whiskers tickle," they say.

Blue hides behind Barb's arm. Then she pops out. *Peekaboo!* One boy makes Blue a car out of building bricks. Blue climbs up on the little car and tries it out. Blue likes climbing, but she likes making friends best.

Blue the friendly rat

Blue

BREED: Dumbo Fancy Rat

AGE: 1 year

COLOR: blue

WEIGHT: 11 ounces

FAVORITE FOOD: Cheerios

FAVORITE PLAYMATE: her sisters

LIVES IN: New York

Great blessings belong to those who are humble.

—MATTHEW 5:5

20
Cori

Sometimes it's hard to be the younger sibling. Especially when your older sis is super smart and talented. And, especially when you are the little sister who is just learning. But Cori the retriever has a special talent too, and a purpose all her own.

Cori lives in sunny California with Judy and Surf Dog Ricochet. Ricochet is famous for helping kids with different needs surf. Cori has a wonderful gift, too.

When she was just a very young pup, Cori went out to the big, sparkly swimming pool in the backyard with her family. Ricochet jumped right in. Ricochet is used to the pool and swimming. She loves being in the water. Cori didn't jump in. She just dipped a paw over the edge. She was afraid. "It's okay, Cori," Judy said. "You just wait until you're ready."

One day some teenagers came over to swim. Cori relaxed by the side of the pool. But when the kids dove underwater, Cori whined. She was worried about them. She ran to the edge of the pool and barked. When the kids popped back up, she stopped barking. Another day a little girl was splashing around in the pool. She was having fun, but Cori must have thought she was in trouble. She jumped right in and tried to rescue the girl.

"Now you are ready," Judy said, with a proud smile.

It wasn't long before Cori learned to feel comfortable in the water. It seemed that she wanted all children to feel comfortable in the water, too. Whenever she met frightened children, she jumped into the pool and swam next to them. Judy realized that there were kids Cori could help. Many autistic children are attracted to sparkly water. They need to learn to swim in case they accidentally fall in. Other kids have diseases that weaken their muscles. Swimming is good for them, but they don't know how to swim. There are also children who don't like the feel of water or being wet. They are all afraid to go into the water, just as Cori was when she was a puppy.

Now, the gentle retriever doggy-paddles beside kids with extra needs. "Do you want to swim with Cori?" Judy asks a timid girl who has come to meet them. The girl has trouble learning things and doing things alone. She's also very afraid of the water. Judy throws a ball into the pool. Cori jumps right in and retrieves the ball. Then, the girl throws the ball. Cori jumps into the pool. They do this a few times, and Cori makes it look like fun.

Next, it is time for the girl to get in the water. She's still anxious, even with her mom wading beside her. "Cori will help you," Judy says. Cori wears a lifejacket with a handle on the back. "Just hang onto the handle." Cori paddles her strong legs, towing the child in the water. "I'm doing it!" the girl says. When she's with Cori, she's not afraid.

Then Judy points to a long pole with foam circles on each end. It looks like a dumbbell floating in the pool. "Can you hold the bar and kick your feet?" Judy asks. The girl doesn't want to do it. Cori jumps into the pool, holds the bar with her teeth, and moves her legs. *This is how you do it.* The girl laughs and holds the bar and kicks.

The swimming lessons go well. But the girl is still afraid to go underwater. "Watch Cori," Judy says. Cori swims underwater. When she comes up for air, everyone cheers. "Okay, I'll try," the girl says. She feels brave with Cori next

Cori

BREED: Golden Retriever–Yellow Lab mix

AGE: 1 ½ years

COLOR: yellow

WEIGHT: 55 lbs.

FAVORITE FOOD: Cheetos

FAVORITE TOY: retrieving ball

LIVES IN: California

to her. First, she ducks her head under, just a little bit. Then her shoulders. The rest of her follows. She pops out of the water grinning and pumping her fist.

Swimming class is over, and the girl gets out of the pool. Cori shakes, droplets of water flying everywhere. Everyone gets wet, but it's okay. That's just what dogs do. Now it's time for a snack and a nap—a couple of Cori's favorite things. That, and a hug from Judy. A perfect day—a swim with a friend, relaxing by the pool, and a job well done.

Encourage those who are
afraid. Help those who are weak.
Be patient with everyone.

—1 Thessalonians 5:14

21
Harley

Some animals help kids. Some animals heal kids. And some animals hug kids. And hugging is exactly what Harley does best.

Harley is visiting a summer camp. The campers are sitting in a circle in the grass. They're there to learn about nature and their world. But here comes an animal they don't usually see. "Say hello to Harley," a woman named Deb says. Harley is bigger than a dog but smaller than a horse.

Harley is an alpaca. An alpaca is a relative of a llama. Alpacas come in twenty-two colors, including black, brown, and tan. Harley is pure white. He has black eyes and a pink nose. His hooves are like a camel's—they have a split toe and a soft pad on the bottom. There are no wild alpacas. They are all tame and kept as pets, and raised mainly for their thick, warm wool.

"Are you ready for your hug?" Deb asks. A little girl in blue striped shorts jumps up. She throws her arms around Harley's neck. Harley leans against her and nuzzles her cheek. This is his way of hugging. His hug is soft and warm.

The girl looks at Harley. He closes his eyes, scrunches his face and curls his lip. She makes a face back at him. Harley looks as if he's smiling at her. There are few things quite as silly as making funny faces with an alpaca. All the campers take turns patting and hugging Harley.

Sometimes Harley is shy. Alpacas can be timid until they get to know you. Then, he is friendly and curious. He sniffs the girl all over. This is one way he collects information about people and things in his world. He makes a noise, almost like a baby crying, but not so sad. "It sounds like he's humming," the girl says.

"Yes, that is because he wants to get to know you," Deb says.

The girl leans in close. "My name is Leah," she says, "and I like to jump rope."

Harley doesn't travel alone. Deb lives with and loves a whole bunch of animals. They are all therapy animals, and they visit people who need them. What a sight! Deb has a big furry white dog, almost as big as Harley. There's also a fluffy cat. Deb pushes a cart and all the smaller animals hop on for a ride. There's a bunny, a guinea pig, a duck, a

Harley the lovable alpaca

cockatiel, and an albino skunk. All the animals go together and visit libraries, schools, nursing homes, hospitals, and summer programs, too.

When Deb walks in with her animals, the kids are surprised. None of the animals are in cages. They all sit next to each other. Or on top of each other. Sometimes the bird perches on the cat. They don't fight. Harley walks next to the big dog. He is friends with the dog.

If all these different animals get along, the kids think, then we can too.

Harley

BREED: Alpaca

AGE: 10 years

COLOR: white

WEIGHT: 165 lbs.

FAVORITE FOOD: grass

FAVORITE TOY: doesn't play with toys

LIVES IN: Illinois

Then wolves will live at peace with lambs, and leopards will lie down in peace with young goats. Calves, lions, and bulls will all live together in peace.

—Isaiah 11:6

How Children Can Help Animals

Your family dog. Your grandma's cat. The goldfish in your classroom. A bird on a branch. All animals are special. God makes them so. Just as he made you special. Animals give us so much, it's up to us to give back to them and treat them well.

1 Handle all animals gently and kindly. They can feel pain, just like you.

2 Always tell an adult if you see an animal in need, or anyone being unkind to animals.

3 Give an animal a second chance. Adopt a dog, cat, rabbit, or other pet from a shelter or rescue group.

4 Ask your parents about *fostering* an animal—caring for a dog or cat at your house until it finds a forever home.

5 Give your pets something to do. Play with them often. You are their favorite toy.

6 Pick up trash on paths and beaches that might harm wildlife.

7 Care for your pets joyfully. Feed, walk, brush, and clean up after them. After all, they are part of the family.

8 Buy an extra bag or can of pet food and donate it to your local food pantry. Or start a pet food drive at your school or church.

9 Volunteer to help animals at a shelter, wildlife refuge, or anywhere.

10 Share your love of animals with your friends, so they can help too.

Acknowledgments

A heartfelt thank you to all the kids, families, and handlers who shared their stories for this book, and a hug to each one of your animals (also a marshmallow, strawberry, or biscuit) to thank them for inspiring us all. A huge thank you to Mike for always being by my side—you're so devoted, you could almost be a Golden Retriever; Jon Sweeney and the wonderful folks at Paraclete Press; my proofreaders Susan Karas and Stephanie Thompson; and all the Marbleshapers for your support. And a special thank you to service, therapy, and support animals, and loving pets who give their all every day to make the world a better place for us.

Resources

4 Paws for Ability	www.4pawsforability.org
American Humane	www.americanhumane.org
Animal Health Foundation	www.animalhealthfoundation.net
Bacon Bits	www.facebook.com/Bacon-Bits
Bunnies in Baskets	www.bunniesinbaskets.org
Exceptional Equestrians of the Missouri Valley	www.eemv.org
Gentle Carousel Miniature Therapy Horses	www.gentlecarouseltherapyhorses.com
Green Chimneys	www.greenchimneys.org
Gracie the Therapy Cat	www.facebook.com/Graciethetherapycat
Healing Whiskers	www.healingwhiskers.com
JoJo Comfort Dog	www.facebook.com/JoJoComfortDog
Keep Kids Fire Safe	www.keepkidsfiresafe.org
K-9 comfort	www.facebook.com/k9comfort
Lentil	www.mynameislentil.com
Lutheran Church Charities	www.lutheranchurchcharities.org
Pet Partners	www.petpartners.org
Murfy the Therapy Dog	www.facebook.com/LoveMurfy
Paws with a Cause	www.pawswithacause.org
Paws Giving Independence	www.givingindependence.org
Puppy Prodigies	www.puppyprodigies.org
Raul the Therapy Cat	www.facebook.com/raulthetherapycat
Sheldon and Spencer	www.facebook.com/sheldonspencer.barry
Surf Dog Ricochet	www.SurfDogRicochet.com
Therapy Dogs International	www.tdi-dog.org

About the Author

Peggy Frezon is contributing editor of *All Creatures* magazine and regular contributor to *Guideposts* magazine and *Chicken Soup for the Soul* books. She is also the author of books about the human-animal bond, including *Faithfully Yours: The Amazing Bond Between Us and the Animals We Love.* Peggy grew up with dogs, cats, guinea pigs, rabbits, hamsters, gerbils, turtles and goldfish. She and her husband rescue senior Golden Retrievers and do therapy dog work together. They share their home with two faithful Goldens, Ernest and Petey. Connect with Peggy at www.peggyfrezon. com and on Facebook at https://www.facebook.com /PeggyFrezonBooks.

You may also be interested in...

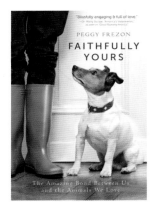

Faithfully Yours
The Amazing Bond Between Us and the Animals We Love
Peggy Frezon

ISBN 978-1-61261-602-5 | $17.99

Stories of devotion, protection, healing, compassion, and faith, between animals and their human companions.

Keller's Heart
John Gray, illustrated by Shanna Brickell

ISBN 978-1-64060-174-1 | $12.99

The story of a special girl named Raven and a special dog named Keller who rescue each other, become best friends, and show those around them that it is OK to be different and that everyone needs a friend.

Available at bookstores
Paraclete Press | 1-800-451-5006
www.paracletepress.com